Dormet

Dormet

Healthy recipes for the college cook

McKenzie L. Amaral

ISBN: 1984136550
ISBN 13: 9781984136558
Library of Congress Control Number: 2018900976
CreateSpace Independent Publishing Platform
North Charleston, South Carolina

Contents

Snacks and Sweets

Kitchen Tools

Some tools essential for making gourmet-*Dormet*!

Cutting board

Bowl

Fork

Knife

Measuring cups

Microwave

Spoon

Toaster

Optional: portable griddle

Introduction

*D*ormet aims to bring the gourmet to college cuisine. *Dormet* is a cookbook that offers a unique combination of easy, healthy, and quick recipes for every college student.

Before I began college, I was accustomed to fabulous food and fresh ingredients. Growing up in California's wine country, the Napa Valley, I was minutes away from some of the best restaurants in the world and the freshest fruits and vegetables you can find. I grew up learning how to cook with the best ingredients and knowing the importance of a balanced diet through my exposure to this five-star cuisine.

When I was thirteen years old, I was sick. My sickness didn't allow me to be a normal teenager; I couldn't be as active as I would have liked or even go to school. I was only thirteen, but I had an eating disorder. My sickness plagued me for just under a year, led me to many doctors and out of school, but ultimately guided me to become a stronger version of myself. My eating disorder made me a skeleton of myself, stripped me of who I was, and wore my body down physically but even more so mentally.

Having this experience of an eating disorder, I was exposed to the true value that food holds and the importance of food not only for the body but also for the soul.

I had always been interested in cooking, but after my battle with anorexia, I had a newfound knowledge of nutrition and the importance of a balanced diet. By using nutritious whole ingredients and having a dorm room for a kitchen, I was able to satisfy my gourmet appetite with my college-student lifestyle by integrating my knowledge of fresh food and nutrition in an innovative way. Food is supposed to be fun and an enjoyable experience, and when I started college, the pleasure of cooking was sacrificed as I stood in the cafeteria line waiting for reheated stale food.

The recipes in this book include everything from pancakes to pasta—all with a healthy spin. I believe in eating fresh whole foods that nurture not only your body but also your soul. As a college student, I have realized students do not have time to cook for thirty minutes, so all the recipes take ten minutes or less to prepare—making it possible for any college student to bring gourmet food into his or her dorm room.

This book provides recipes for one; however, you can double or triple the recipes to feed envious roommates!

Eat healthy, be healthy, and bon appétit!

Breakfast

Muesli

A perfect on-the-go meal—put it in a mason jar, and enjoy!

Ingredients

1 cup rolled oats
1 cup milk of your choice (Almond milk adds some sweetness)
Spoonful of Greek yogurt
Handful of walnuts
½ apple

Appliances

Bowl
Knife

Prep time: 5 minutes
Cook/soak time: 8 hours

Step 1
Place one cup of oats in a bowl.

Step 2
Pour one cup of milk in the bowl with oats and place paper towel over oats.

Step 3
Cover oats and milk overnight.

Step 4
After soaking overnight, place a spoonful of yogurt on oats.

Step 5
Cut apple in thin slices and sprinkle apple and walnuts on oats.

OATMEAL YOUR OWN WAY

Oatmeal is a nutritious way to start your day and can match your morning mood.

Ingredients

1 cup rolled oats
1½ cups water

Appliances

Bowl

Time: 4 minutes

Step 1
Place oats and water in a bowl, and place paper towel on top of the bowl.

Step 2
Microwave for 2 minutes.

Step 3
Mix and match some of the following toppings:

Almonds, flaxseed, banana
Walnuts, blueberries
Shredded coconut, banana, blueberries
Cranberries, walnuts

Sweetener tip: use pure maple syrup instead of brown sugar, maple syrup is natural and doesn't have any additives.

ALMOND BUTTER AND TOAST

Ingredients

2 spoonfuls of almond butter
2 slices of your preferred bread (Honey whole wheat is a favorite of mine!)
1 banana

Appliances

Toaster
Knife

Time: 2 minutes

Step 1
Toast bread in a toaster.

Step 2
Spread almond butter on the toast.

Step 3
Slice banana on top of the almond butter.

Oatmeal-Blueberry-Banana Pancakes

A healthy spin on your average pancake make these a guilt-free indulgence!

Ingredients

1½ cups oats
Pinch of salt
¼ cup water
2 tablespoons coconut oil
1 tablespoon coconut oil for griddle
1 tablespoon maple syrup
1 small banana
½ cup blueberries

Appliances

Griddle
Mixing bowl

Time: 10 minutes

Step 1
Mix oats, salt, water, coconut oil, maple syrup, and banana in bowl.

Step 2
Slowly mix in blueberries.

Step 3
Place coconut oil on hot griddle and pour the batter on the griddle so each pancake is about 5 inches across.

Step 4
Cook pancakes until golden brown on each side.

Eggs 101

Scrambled

Crack eggs into a bowl.

(Egg hack: use the eggs shell to grab any parts of eggs that cracked into bowl.)

Scramble with fork, mixing the yolk and egg white together.

Either microwave for 2 minutes, or pour eggs onto griddle.

Sprinkle in salt and pepper and maybe a touch of cheddar cheese for an extra kick!

Poached

Fill a bowl halfway full with water.

Crack one egg into water, making sure it is submerged in water.

Cover with plate.

Microwave for 1 minute.

Check the egg. A properly poached egg should have a firm egg white and runny yolk.

If you would like a more cooked egg, microwave for 30 more seconds.

Sunny-Side Up

Spray a microwaveable plate with olive or coconut oil.

Crack egg onto plate, and poke yolk with fork.

Microwave for 45 seconds.

Hard-Boiled Eggs

Fill a bowl ¾ way full of water.

Microwave for 3 minutes.

Poke the bottom of egg with a safety pin or thumbtack.

Place the egg into the hot water, and cover with a plate.

Microwave for 4 minutes.

Check the egg. If you would like it more cooked, leave the egg in the water for 2 more minutes.

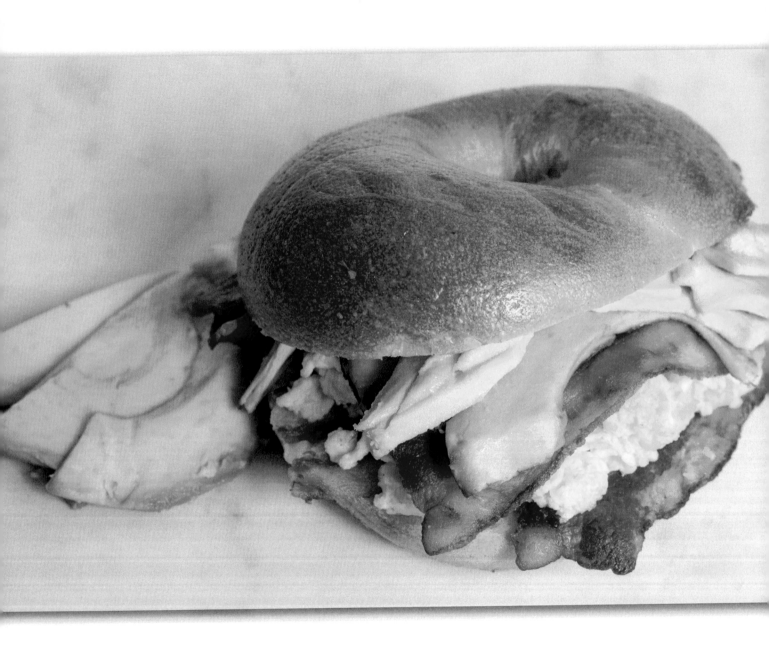

Bondy's Eggcellent Breakfast

My college roommate and I enjoyed this breakfast sandwich any day of the week and any time of the day!

Ingredients

2 slices of sourdough bread or a bagel
2 eggs
3 strips of bacon

Appliances

Toaster
Microwave

Time: 4 minutes

Step 1
Wrap bacon in a paper towel, and place in the microwave for 3 minutes.

Step 2
Place bread in the toaster.

Step 3
Choose the style of your eggs, see Eggs 101.

Step 4
Place eggs on toast, and stack bacon on top.

Avocado is a delicious addition!

Avocado Toast and Poached Eggs

One of my all-time favorites (with the egg or without the egg) is avocado and toast.

Ingredients

½ avocado
2 slices of your favorite bread
2 eggs
2 cups of water
Salt
Pepper

Appliances

Toaster
Microwave

Time: 5 minutes

Step 1
Mash avocado.

Step 2
See Eggs 101 on how to poach eggs.

Step 3
Toast bread.

Step 4
Spread avocado on the toast.

Step 5
Place eggs on the toast and sprinkle with salt and pepper.

Lunch and Dinner

Open-Faced Sandwich

Ingredients
½ avocado
½ tomato
Handful of goat cheese
1 slice of your favorite bread
Roasted chicken breast

Appliances
Knife

Time: 3 minutes

Step 1
Mash avocado, and spread it on the bread. (You may toast the bread, if you prefer.)

Step 2
Slice tomato, and place it on top of the avocado.

Step 3
Crumble cheese over the tomato.

Step 4
Layer chicken breast over the cheese.

Sweet-potato or vegetable chips make the perfect side!

BRIE, PEAR, AND PROSCIUTTO SANDWICH

Lunch, dinner, or dessert? You decide!

Ingredients

3–4 slices of brie cheese
1 pear
3 slices of prosciutto
½ baguette

Appliances

Knife

Time: 2 minutes

Step 1
Slice baguette down the length of the bread.

Step 2
Evenly place brie along the length of baguette.
Option: place baguette and brie in toaster.

Step 3
Layer prosciutto and pears over brie.

For an extra delight, drizzle honey over the brie.

McKenzie L. Amaral

PESTO PASTA WITH SAUSAGE

Craving pasta but not sure if it's possible to make in the room you are calling your home? Here's how to whip up a warm bowl of fresh tortellini with pesto!

Ingredients

2 cups tortellini
¼ cup pesto
Sausage (chicken-apple sausage adds a nice flavor)

Appliances

Microwave
Bowl
Optional: griddle for sausage

Prep time: 2 minutes
Cook time: 4 minutes

Step 1
Slice sausage into thin circles.

Step 2
Place tortellini in bowl, and fill the bowl with enough water to cover the tortellini, microwave for 3 minutes.

Step 3
Place sliced sausage in microwave for 1 minute, or place on hot griddle, flipping after 1 minute.

Step 4
Drizzle pesto over the hot tortellini, mixing as you drizzle. Add sausage, and mix together.

Chicken-Apple Salad

Ingredients
Handful of greens (Kale is a favorite of mine.)
1 apple
1 pre-cooked chicken breast (Rotisserie chickens are a great option!)
½ cup brown rice
½ lemon

Appliances
Bowl
Knife

Prep time: 2 minutes
Cook time: 15 minutes

Step 1
In a bowl, place ½ cup rice and 1 cup water.

Step 2
Microwave, uncovered, for 15 minutes or until the water is absorbed.

Step 3
When rice is cooked, mix in kale, apple, and chicken breast.

Step 4
Squeeze lemon over salad for a citrusy kick, and enjoy!

HUMMUS-CUCUMBER PITA POCKETS

A camping recipe from a weekend trip I took to Oklahoma, which turned into one of my favorite recipes!

Ingredients

¼ cup hummus
1 cucumber
1 pita bread

Appliances

Knife

Time: 2 minutes

Step 1
Slice pita bread open.

Step 2
Slice cucumber into circles, and then cut each circle into quarters (four pieces).

Step 3
Spread hummus inside the pita pocket.

Step 4
Sprinkle cucumber pieces inside the pita pocket.

QUINOA

Quinoa is a nutritious base to any meal. Add some vegetables, and you'll have a nutritious meal in minutes!

Ingredients

1 cup quinoa
2 cups water

Appliances

Bowl

Time: 18 minutes

Step 1
Add quinoa and water to bowl.

Step 2
Cover the bowl with a paper towel or plastic wrap, and place the bowl in a microwave. Heat for 6 minutes.

Step 3
Remove bowl, uncover, and stir.

Step 4
Recover the bowl, and place back in microwave for 2 minutes.

Step 5
Remove the bowl, and keep it covered for 5–10 minutes.

QUINOA, SWEET POTATO, AND BLACK-BEAN BOWL
Chipotle has nothing on this nutritious and delicious burrito bowl!

Ingredients
1 cup quinoa
1 sweet potato
½ cup canned seasoned black beans
Handful of greens (kale or spinach)

Appliances
Bowl
Knife
Microwave

Prep time: 3 minutes
Cook time: 10 minutes

Step 1
Cook quinoa (see quinoa recipe).

Step 2
Poke holes in sweet potato, and microwave for 3 minutes. Flip. Microwave opposite side for 3 more minutes.

Step 3
Microwave black beans for 45 seconds.

Step 4
Place greens in a bowl, slowly mix in quinoa, and sprinkle with sweet potatoes and black beans.

Spinach-Broccoli-Pesto Quinoa

Ingredients

1 cup quinoa
1 cup spinach
½ cup frozen broccoli
1 tablespoon pesto

Appliances

Bowl

Prep time: 3 minutes
Cook time: 20 minutes

Step 1
Cook quinoa (see quinoa recipe).

Step 2
Microwave broccoli for 2 minutes.

Step 3
While the quinoa is still hot, slowly mix in pesto and spinach leaves.

Step 4
Sprinkle in broccoli, and add spinach for a garnish.

ZUCCHINI NOODLES WITH A TWIST

A healthy spin to satisfy your pasta needs.

Ingredients

Zucchini noodles (Trader Joe's and Veggie Noodle Co. are my favorites.)

2 eggs

Salt and pepper, to taste

Optional: ¼ cup marinara or pesto sauce

Appliances

Microwave

Griddle or egg griddle

Time: 8 minutes

Step 1

Place noodles in a bowl, and microwave for 2 minutes.

Step 2

Cook eggs in desired style, see Eggs 101.

Step 3

Take zucchini noodles out of the microwave, and place eggs on top.

Step 4

Sprinkle salt and pepper over eggs.

Step 5

Optional: to make these noodles extra saucy, add ¼ cup of marinara or pesto sauce.

VEGGIE-BURGER BOWL

Sometimes I have a need for greens, and this veggie-burger bowl meets that need every time.

Ingredients

1 frozen veggie burger
Lettuce of choice
Handful of frozen broccoli
Avocado
½ sweet potato

Appliances

Microwave
1 bowls
Knife

Time: 10 minutes

Step 1
Microwave sweet potato on high for 5 minutes.

Step 2
Microwave veggie burger for 3 minutes.

Step 3
Place broccoli in a bowl, and fill it with water. Microwave for 2 minutes.

Step 4
Place lettuce and broccoli in a bowl, put veggie burger on top, and spread avocado on patty.

SAUCY SAUSAGE SALAD

Ingredients
Chicken sausage
Lettuce of choice (I like a kale-spinach mix.)
Cucumber

Appliances
Microwave or griddle
Knife
Bowl

Time: 4 minutes

Step 1
Slice sausage into rounds.

Step 2
Place sausage on griddle or in a microwave for 60 seconds.

Step 3
Slice cucumber.

Step 4
Toss the cucumber, lettuce, and sausage in a bowl.

365-Day Salad Dressing

It's called 365 for a reason—this salad dressing is perfect for every day of the year.

Ingredients

2 tablespoons olive oil
1 teaspoon vinegar
1 teaspoon jam
½ a lemon, juiced

Appliances

Bowl
Fork

Time: 2 minutes

Step 1
Mix all the ingredients in a bowl.

Step 2
Whisk until all the ingredients are combined.

Step 3
Pour on greens of your choice and enjoy!

Snacks and Sweets

Banana-Blueberry Bites

Ingredients
1 banana
¼ cup almond butter
Handful of blueberries

Appliances
Knife

Time: 2 minutes

Step 1
Peel and slice banana.

Step 2
Spread almond butter on the banana slices.

Step 3
Place blueberries on top of almond butter.

No-Bake Energy Bites

These delicious bites taste like cookie dough but are wholesome, with nut butter and flaxseed.

Ingredients

1 cup oats
½ cup chocolate chips
½ cup flaxseed
½ cup shredded coconut
½ cup nut butter of your choice (e.g., almond butter)
⅓ cup honey or maple syrup
1 teaspoon vanilla extract

Appliances

Bowl

Time: 5 minutes

Step 1
Place all ingredients in a bowl.

Step 2
Mix thoroughly.

Step 3
Using a tablespoon, scoop dough, round it into balls (using your hands to shape, if you prefer), and place on the plate.

Step 4
Enjoy! Or cover, place in refrigerator, and enjoy throughout the week!

Cinnamon-Flaxseed Muffin

Perfect for breakfast, a snack, or an after-dinner indulgence!

Ingredients

¼ cup ground flaxseed
1 teaspoon cinnamon
1 egg
1 tablespoon coconut oil
1 teaspoon baking powder
1 teaspoon of sugar

Appliances

Mug

Time: 2 minutes

Step 1
Mix all the ingredients in the mug. Make sure to scrape the bottom and sides.

Step 2
Microwave for 1 minute. Check to see if the muffin appears wet in the center; if so, cook for an additional 15 seconds.

Step 3
Shake the muffin out, or just eat it out of the mug. Enjoy!

APPLE PIZZAS

Ingredients
1 apple
Mix and match handfuls of the following toppings:
Almond butter
Chia seeds
Coconut
Dried cranberries
Chocolate chips

Appliances
Knife

Time: 2 minutes

Step 1
Slice apple in rounds.

Step 2
Spread almond butter on apple slices.

Step 3
Sprinkle coconut, chia seeds, cranberries or chocolate chips on apple slices.

Chia Pudding

Ingredients
¼ cup chia seeds
2 cups milk of your choice (Almond is yummy!)
1 teaspoon vanilla extract
¼ cup nuts
¼ cup fresh berries

Appliances
Bowl

Prep time: 1 minute
Cook/soak time: 15 minutes

Step 1
Stir chia seeds and milk in a bowl.

Step 2
Let sit for 15 minutes.

Step 3
Top it with nuts and berries, and enjoy!

Sweetener tip: add cacao powder to your milk for a chocolatey chia!

ALMOND-BUTTER TORTILLA WRAP

Ingredients
2 spoonfuls almond butter
1 whole-wheat tortilla
1 banana

Appliances
Knife

Time: 2 minutes

Step 1
Spread almond butter on tortilla.

Step 2
Slice a banana in small rounds.

Step 3
Place banana on tortilla.

Step 4
Tuck the edges of tortilla into center, and roll it.

SWEET-POTATO CHIPS

Ingredients
1 sweet potato
1 spoonful of olive oil
Dash of cinnamon

Appliances
Knife
Bowl
Paper towel

Time: 5 minutes

Step 1
Slice sweet potatoes into very thin circles.

Step 2
In a bowl, mix slices of sweet potato, olive oil, and cinnamon.

Step 3
Place sweet potatoes on a paper towel in a single layer, and microwave for 3½ to 4 minutes.

Dorm-Made Granola

Ingredients
¼ cup old-fashioned oats
1 tablespoon maple syrup, honey, or agave nectar
1 tablespoon coconut
1 tablespoon walnuts
1 teaspoon cinnamon
2 teaspoons water
2 teaspoons vegetable oil
Pinch of salt

Appliances
Fork
Knife
Mug
Chopping block

Time: 5 minutes

Step 1
Chop walnuts.

Step 2
Thoroughly mix all the ingredients in a mug and microwave for 1½ minutes.

Step 3
Remove the mug from microwave, and stir the ingredients again, making sure to scrape sides.

Step 4
Microwave for 1 minute or until oats are golden brown, let stand for 2–3 minutes, and enjoy!

Made in the USA
Lexington, KY
19 October 2018